# Quick

*Griddled kebabs in under 30 mins*
Lamb souvlaki with pickled lettuce, page 110

*Fast food with loads of flavour*
Jacket potatoes with smoked trout, page 86

*Speedy steak with salad and salsa*
Italian-style beef with potato salad, page 100

*Spicy fish in a flash*
Tandoori salmon with lime pickle yogurt, page 34

# WW kitchen collection

## Quick

# The small print

**EGGS** We use medium eggs, unless otherwise stated. Pregnant women, the elderly and children should avoid recipes with eggs which are not fully cooked or raw.

**FRUIT AND VEGETABLES** Recipes use medium-sized fruit and veg, unless otherwise stated.

**REDUCED FAT SOFT CHEESE** Where a recipe uses reduced fat soft cheese, we mean a soft cheese with 30% less fat than its full fat equivalent.

**LOW FAT SPREAD** When a recipe uses a low fat spread, we mean a spread with a fat content of no more than 39%.

**MICROWAVES** If we have used a microwave in any of our recipes, the timings will be for an 850 watt microwave oven.

**PREP AND COOKING TIMES** These are approximate and meant to be guidelines. Prep time includes all the steps up to and following the main cooking time(s). Cooking times may vary according to your oven.

**GLUTEN FREE** The use of the term 'gluten free' or the 'gluten free icon' is illustrative only. Weight Watchers is not responsible for the presence of gluten in the dishes that have not been prepared in accordance with instructions; nor is it responsible for gluten contamination due to an external cause. Recipes labelled as gluten free, or displaying the gluten free icon, only include ingredients that naturally do not contain gluten. Whenever using canned, bottled or other types of packaged processed ingredients, such as sauces and stocks, it is essential to check that those ingredients do not contain gluten.

**SmartPoints** have been calculated using the values for generic foods, not brands (except where stated). Tracking using branded items may affect the recorded SmartPoints.

# Seven.

Produced by Seven Publishing on behalf of Weight Watchers International, Inc. Published October 2016. All rights reserved. No part of this publication may be reproduced, stored in a retrieval system or transmitted in any form by any means, electronic, mechanical photocopying, recording or otherwise, without the prior written permission of Seven Publishing.

First published in Great Britain by Seven Publishing Ltd. Copyright © 2016, Weight Watchers International, Inc.

Seven Publishing Ltd
3-7 Herbal Hill
London
EC1R 5EJ
www.seven.co.uk

This book is copyright under the Berne Convention. No reproduction without permission. All rights reserved.

10 9 8 7 6 5 4 3 2 1

Weight Watchers SmartPoints and the SmartPoints icon are the registered trademarks of Weight Watchers International, Inc and are used under license by Weight Watchers (UK) Ltd. All rights reserved.

A CIP catalogue record for this book is available from the British Library. ISBN: 978-0-9935835-2-0

**WEIGHT WATCHERS PUBLICATIONS TEAM** Imogen Prescott, Samantha Rees, Nicola Kirk, Stephanie Williams, Danielle Smith

**THANKS TO WEIGHT WATCHERS AUSTRALASIA**

**PHOTOGRAPHY** Steve Brown, Andy Lewis, Vanessa Levis, Alex Luck, Rob Palmer, John Paul Urizar

**RECIPES** Alexandra Elliott, Chrissy Freer, Sarah Hobbs, Kathy Knudsen, Kirrily La Rosa, Cathie Lonnie, Gemma Luongo, Liz Macri, Lucy Nunes, Tracy Rutherford

**STYLING** Julz Beresford, Marie-Hélène Clauzon, Sarah Cook, Yael Grinham, Jane Hann, Michelle Noerianto, Luis Peral

**FOR SEVEN PUBLISHING LTD**

**EDITORIAL & DESIGN**
**Editor-in-Chief** Helen Renshaw
**Editor** Ward Hellewell  **Sub-editors** Oliver Fritz, Clare Devane
**Art director** Liz Baird  **Picture editor** Carl Palmer

**ACCOUNT MANAGEMENT**
**Account manager** Jo Brennan  **Business Director, retail** Andy Roughton, **Group publishing director** Kirsten Price

**PRODUCTION**
**Production director** Sophie Dillon
**Colour reproduction** by F1 Colour  **Printed in Italy** by L.E.G.O S.p.A

# Contents

# Want fast food that's healthy?

This book proves that it is not only possible, but easy, too. With the help of some clever tips and tricks, well-chosen ingredients and **speedy cooking** techniques, you'll have no trouble getting a delicious meal on the table in **less than 30 minutes**.

We've brought together some of the **most popular**, quick-to-make recipes from the Weight Watchers kitchen, including meals that are ready in 15 minutes or under – **how's that for fast?**

From soups and salads to stir-fries, pasta, curries and more, there are **quick meal ideas for all seasons**. Every recipe has been tried and tested, and we've worked out all the SmartPoints, making it easy for you to fit them into your eating plan.

---

**LOOK OUT FOR THE SYMBOLS BELOW:**

 The number inside the SmartPoints coin tells you how many SmartPoints are in the serving.

If you're following No Count, you can eat this recipe to your satisfaction without having to count it.

**GF** A recipe that is totally gluten free, or can be made gluten free with a few simple swaps. Always check labels, as some ingredients, such as soy sauce, may contain gluten.

**V** Indicates a recipe that is vegetarian.

# for saving time in the kitchen

With these simple tips and tricks, you can create speedy meals that taste great and will fit into your SmartPoints budget.

### The right ingredients

Some ingredients lend themselves to speedy cooking. When you're in a hurry, choose things that need only light cooking, for example, spinach leaves rather than cabbage. See opposite for more time-saving ingredients.

### Batch cook

When you do have some spare time, consider batch cooking things like pasta sauces, stewed fruits or soups and freezing them for later.

### Use your gadgets

Let your kitchen gadgets do the work for you. A stick blender, food processor or spiraliser can make prepping ingredients super-fast. Even something as humble as a pair of kitchen scissors for snipping herbs will save you precious minutes when you are pressed for time.

### Master your microwave

Don't just use your microwave for heating ready meals – they're also great for quick-cooking vegetables, thawing out frozen meats and even making entire dishes from scratch. Spend some time getting to know your microwave by reading the manual thoroughly, then put it to work, so you don't have to.

### Read the recipe

A few moments spent reading through a recipe before you start cooking can see off any problems and delays later on. Checking you've got all the ingredients, for example, will mean you avoid any unwelcome hiccups halfway through cooking.

### Multi-task

Make the most of your time in the kitchen by figuring out the most efficient way of cooking. For example, rather than prepping all the ingredients before you start, it might make more sense to get one ingredient bubbling away on the hob, while you're chopping the next one.

### Keep it simple

As a rule, recipes that use fewer ingredients are quicker to put together. Why spend ages hunting through your storecupboard and measuring out a dozen different spices, when a single spice mix or curry powder would do just as well? Keep it simple and you'll keep it speedy.

### Preheat your oven

If a recipe calls for your oven, wok or griddle pan to be preheated, do this first. While it's heating up, you can be getting on with preparing your recipe ingredients.

### Double up

A neat time-saving trick if a recipe calls for different types of vegetables, or even pasta and veg, is to cook them in the same pot. You'll have fewer pots on the go – and less washing up afterwards. Stagger the cooking times, starting with whatever takes the longest to cook. For example, if you're cooking pasta and peas together, put the pasta into the pot first, then add the peas a few minutes before the end of the pasta's cooking time.

## Time-saving ingredients

Using ready-prepared or quick-cook ingredients can save you precious time in the kitchen. Here are some indispensable items for your storecupboard and fridge:

### Tinned tomatoes

Great for pasta sauces, pizza toppings, soups, stews and casseroles, tinned tomatoes are the starting point for so many dishes; so make them a storecupboard staple. Choose ready-chopped ones to save even more time, and, if you like, add even more flavour to recipes by choosing varieties that include herbs, garlic or chillies. Reduce them down to make a simple sauce for spiralised courgette 'pasta', or try them in our Quick seafood stew (p40).

### Prepared salads & stir-fries

Salads and stir-fry dishes are super healthy, but all that chopping and grating can take up time in the kitchen. You can keep things quick and easy by choosing ready prepped vegetables, salad bags or stir-fry mixes that can be served on their own or included in recipes such as Tofu & sweet chilli noodles (p64). Remember to check the use-by date when buying, as they'll lose their freshness quicker than unprepped veg.

### Cooked meats

Delicious and easy salads, wraps and sandwiches can be put together in minutes using ready-cooked lean meats such as chicken, beef and ham. You can also speed up other recipes, like our Chicken & ramen noodle soup (p38).

### Fresh pasta & wok-ready noodles

Fresh pasta is ready in a fraction of the time it takes to cook dried pasta, and wok-ready noodles are also a brilliant way to save you time after a busy day. Try Courgette, lemon & ricotta linguine (p36) or Prawn & miso noodle soup (p22).

### Frozen veg

For a near-instant side dish, it's hard to beat frozen vegetables for taste and convenience. They require only minimal cooking – steam them in a little water in the microwave for a really fast fix and jazz them up with fresh herbs, seasoning and a squeeze of lemon. They're also great added to dishes such as Miso fish with spinach rice (p54), Grilled steaks with cauliflower rice (p92) or Baked salmon with quinoa & pea pilaf (p102).

### Tinned pulses & beans

Beans and pulses such as chickpeas and lentils are a healthy and filling way to bulk out dishes. Most require a lengthy cooking process, so using tinned varieties is a great time-saver. Use them in Fast beef chilli con carne (p50) or Maple chicken with butternut houmous (p88). It's a good idea to drain and rinse them before using, as some can contain quite a lot of salt and sugar.

### Microwaveable rice

Think you can't improve on the cooking time for rice? Think again! Microwaveable packs are ready in a couple of minutes and there's a great variety of flavours and types available. Try them in recipes like Teriyaki chicken with pickled ginger salad (p18) or Lamb & black bean stir-fry (p26).

15 minutes & under

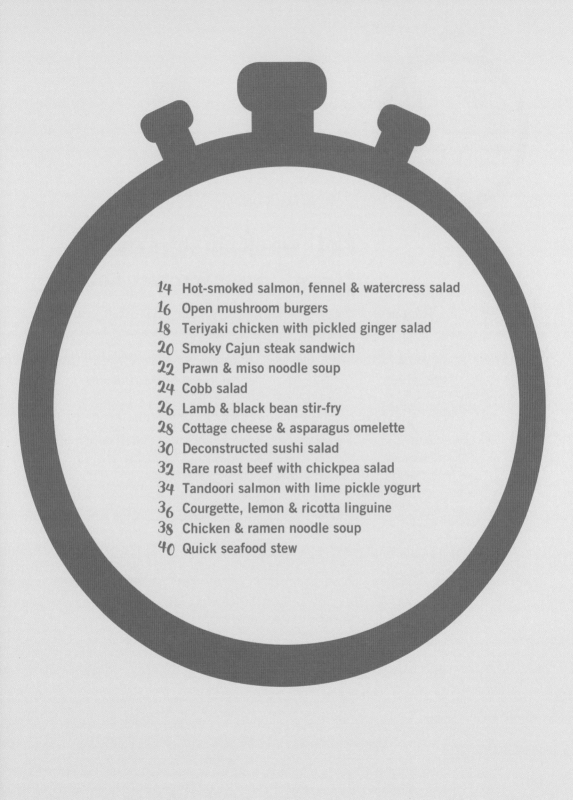

**Cook's tip**

For No Count, use smoked
trout instead of salmon,
and fat free natural yogurt
instead of buttermilk.

15 MINUTES & UNDER

# Hot-smoked salmon, fennel & watercress salad

**Serves 4**

**Prep time**
10 minutes

This simple but delicious salad is ready in a flash.
The watercress adds lots of fresh, peppery flavour.

**Ingredients**

2 baby fennel bulbs, sliced
and fronds reserved
1 small cucumber,
sliced into ribbons
1 red pepper, deseeded
and finely chopped
1 bunch watercress
3 x 150g fillets
hot-smoked salmon,
skin removed, flaked
80ml buttermilk
1 tablespoon lemon juice
1 teaspoon Dijon mustard

1 Combine the sliced fennel, cucumber ribbons, red pepper,
watercress and salmon in a large bowl.

2 Chop the fennel fronds and combine them with the
buttermilk, lemon juice and mustard in a small bowl, then
season to taste. Pour the dressing over the salad and toss
gently to combine, then serve immediately.

**SmartPoints** values per serving 5
**SmartPoints** values per recipe 21

# Open mushroom burgers

This delicious veggie burger is sprinkled with crispy crumbs and topped with creamy goats' cheese.

**Serves 4**

**Prep time**
2 minutes

**Cook time**
8 minutes

### Ingredients
4 large portobello mushrooms
2 x 50g wholemeal bread rolls, split
Calorie controlled cooking spray
2 teaspoons olive oil
35g breadcrumbs made from stale wholemeal bread
1 garlic clove, crushed
1 red chilli, deseeded and finely chopped
2 tablespoons chopped fresh flat-leaf parsley
75g reduced-fat mayonnaise
40g rocket
50g goats' cheese, crumbled

1 Preheat the grill to high and line the grill tray with foil. Put the mushrooms on one half of the tray, and the bread rolls, cut-side up, on the other half. Mist the mushrooms with cooking spray. Grill for 4 minutes, removing the bread rolls once they are toasted. Turn mushrooms and mist the uncooked side. Grill for a further 4 minutes or until tender.

2 Meanwhile, heat the olive oil in a small saucepan over a medium-high heat. Cook the breadcrumbs, stirring for 2-3 minutes or until golden. Add the garlic and chilli and cook, stirring for 1 minute or until fragrant. Remove from the heat and stir in the parsley.

3 Spread the rolls with mayonnaise. Top with the rocket, mushrooms, breadcrumb mixture and cheese, and serve.

**SmartPoints** values per serving 6
**SmartPoints** values per recipe 25

## 15 MINUTES & UNDER

# Teriyaki chicken with pickled ginger salad

A Japanese-style marinade flavours the chicken, which is served with a delicious rice salad.

**Serves 4**

**Prep time**
3 minutes

**Cook time**
7 minutes

### Ingredients

60ml teriyaki sauce (ensure gluten free)

2 teaspoons clear honey

500g skinless mini chicken breast fillets

1 tablespoon olive oil

2 x 250g packs microwaveable brown rice

2 small carrots, peeled and sliced into ribbons

150g mangetout, thinly sliced

2 tablespoons finely shredded pickled ginger, plus 2 teaspoons of the pickling liquid

GF

1 Combine the teriyaki sauce and honey in a large bowl. Pour half into a small jug and set aside. Add the mini chicken breast fillets to the remaining mixture in the bowl and toss to coat.

2 Heat half the oil in a large nonstick frying pan over a medium-high heat. Drain the chicken, reserving the marinade. Cook the mini chicken breast fillets for 2-3 minutes on each side, or until cooked through and no pink remains. Add the reserved marinade and cook, turning for 1 minute, or until the sauce is bubbling.

3 Meanwhile, cook the rice according to the pack instructions. Combine the rice, carrots, mangetout, ginger, pickling liquid and remaining oil in large bowl. Slice the mini fillets in half and serve alongside the salad, with any remaining sauce drizzled over.

**SmartPoints** values per serving 12
**SmartPoints** values per recipe 46

# Smoky Cajun steak sandwich

**Serves 4**

**Prep time**
4 minutes

**Cook time**
6 minutes

Thin minute steaks are so quick to cook and the perfect choice for this speedy deli-style sandwich.

## Ingredients

Calorie controlled cooking spray
1 large red onion, sliced into rings
4 x 125g lean beef minute steaks, fat trimmed
2 teaspoons Cajun seasoning
8 slices thick-sliced calorie controlled bread
1 tablespoon reduced-fat salad dressing
50g rocket
2 tablespoons beetroot dip, such as Sainsbury's Beetroot & Sesame Dip

1 Mist a large griddle pan or barbecue with cooking spray and preheat over a medium-high heat. Put the onion in a medium bowl, and mist with the cooking spray. Sprinkle the steaks with the Cajun seasoning.

2 Cook the onion, turning, for 3-4 minutes or until browned. Meanwhile, cook the steaks for 1 minute each side or until cooked to your liking.

3 Meanwhile, toast the bread and spread the dressing over half of the slices. Top with the rocket, steaks, onion and dip. Top with the remaining bread slices and serve.

**SmartPoints** values per serving 8
**SmartPoints** values per recipe 32

**Inside info**

Crispy fried onions add crunch and flavour. You can find them in most big supermarkets.

**15 MINUTES & UNDER**

# Prawn & miso noodle soup

**Serves 4**

**Prep time**
6 minutes

**Cook time**
4 minutes

This easy Asian-style soup includes pak choi, but you could use other green veg, such as spinach.

### Ingredients
**500g raw prawns, peeled with tails on**
**400g wok-ready udon noodles**
**100g miso paste**
**2 bunches pak choi**
**6 spring onions, trimmed and thinly sliced**
**25g crispy fried onion**

1 Fill and boil the kettle. Pour 1.5 litres boiling water into a large saucepan and return to the boil over a medium heat. Add the prawns and noodles, and cook for 3 minutes or until the prawns have turned pink and the noodles have softened.

2 Meanwhile, transfer about a cup of the cooking liquid to a bowl. Whisk in the miso paste until dissolved. Return the miso mixture to the pan with the pak choi and half the spring onions. Cook for 1 minute or until the pak choi has wilted.

3 Ladle the soup into serving bowls. Sprinkle with the fried onion and remaining spring onions to serve.

**SmartPoints** values per serving 9
**SmartPoints** values per recipe 34

**Try this**
You could serve this with a slice of calorie controlled bread – add an extra 1 SmartPoint per 22g slice.

**15 MINUTES & UNDER**

# Cobb salad

A popular dish in America, this easy chicken and bacon salad is a great choice for a quick lunch.

**Serves 4**

**Prep time**
5 minutes
**Cook time**
10 minutes

**Ingredients**
4 eggs
Calorie controlled
cooking spray
5 slices Weight Watchers
Unsmoked Extra Trimmed
Back Bacon, chopped
2 little gem lettuce, chopped
200g cherry tomatoes,
chopped
1 avocado, peeled, stone
removed and diced
2 x 150g cooked skinless
chicken breasts, cubed
80ml reduced-fat
salad dressing
(ensure gluten free)

1 Boil the eggs in a pan of boiling water for 5 minutes. Drain and cool under running cold water, then peel and cut in half. This can be done ahead of time, if you like.

2 Mist a frying pan with cooking spray and put over a medium-high heat. Add the bacon and cook for 5 minutes, stirring, or until browned.

3 Arrange the bacon, lettuce, tomatoes, avocado, chicken and eggs in serving bowls; drizzle with the dressing and serve.

**SmartPoints** values per serving 7
**SmartPoints** values per recipe 28

# Lamb & black bean stir-fry

**Serves 4**

**Prep time**
5 minutes

**Cook time**
10 minutes

Stir-fries are a great choice for quick meals. This one uses lamb mince and plenty of fresh vegetables.

## Ingredients

2 teaspoons olive oil
400g lean lamb mince
200g pack Tenderstem
broccoli and green beans,
cut into bite-size pieces
2 red peppers, deseeded
and chopped
175g babycorn, halved
1 red onion, sliced
2 x 250g packs
microwaveable brown rice
150g black bean sauce
(ensure gluten free)
1 teaspoon cornflour

1 Heat a wok over a high heat. Add the olive oil and heat for 20 seconds, then add the lamb mince and stir-fry for 3-4 minutes or until browned. Add all the vegetables and stir-fry for 4-5 minutes.

2 Meanwhile, cook the rice according to the pack instructions. Mix the black bean sauce with the cornflour and 60ml water in a small bowl until smooth. Add the sauce mixture to the wok and stir-fry for 1 minute or until heated through. Serve the stir-fry with the rice in serving bowls.

SmartPoints values per serving 14
SmartPoints values per recipe 56

# Cottage cheese & asparagus omelette

*Serves 4*

*Prep time*
5 minutes

*Cook time*
7 minutes

Fancy a quick and tasty brunch? This vegetarian omelette with cottage cheese is the perfect choice.

## Ingredients

Calorie controlled cooking spray
2 bunches asparagus, trimmed and cut into 3cm lengths
8 eggs, plus 2 egg whites
80ml skimmed milk
2 tablespoons finely chopped fresh chives
2 tablespoons finely chopped fresh flat-leaf parsley
100g low-fat cottage cheese
75g roasted red peppers (not in oil), sliced

1  Mist a large nonstick frying pan with the cooking spray and place on a high heat. Add the asparagus and cook, stirring, for 2-3 minutes or until just tender. Transfer the asparagus to a plate.

2  Meanwhile, whisk the eggs, egg whites, milk, chives and parsley in a large jug until combined. Season to taste.

3  Mist the same frying pan with cooking spray and reduce the heat to medium-high. Add half the egg mixture and swirl to thinly coat the base of the pan. Cook for 1-2 minutes or until just set. Sprinkle half the omelette with half the asparagus, cottage cheese and red peppers. Fold to enclose the filling. Transfer to a plate and cover to keep warm.

4  Repeat with the remaining egg mixture, asparagus, cottage cheese and red peppers to make one more omelette. Cut the omelettes in half and serve immediately.

**SmartPoints** values per serving 4
**SmartPoints** values per recipe 17

**Inside info**

Mirin is a sweet rice wine used in Asian cooking – you can find it in most supermarkets.

## 15 MINUTES & UNDER

*Serves 4*

*Prep time*
12 minutes

*Cook time*
3 minutes

# Deconstructed sushi salad

You'll get all the delicious flavours of sushi, but without any of the hard work in this easy salad.

*Ingredients*
1 x 250g pack microwaveable brown rice
2 carrots, peeled
1 cucumber
1 toasted nori sheet
½ small avocado
1 teaspoon sesame seeds
2cm-piece fresh ginger, finely grated
1 tablespoon mirin
1 tablespoon light soy sauce
1 teaspoon caster sugar
½ teaspoon sesame oil
½ teaspoon wasabi paste
2 x 185g tins tuna in spring water, drained and flaked
50g pea shoots

**1** Cook the rice according to the pack instructions. Put in a large bowl and set aside for 10 minutes to cool.

**2** Meanwhile, cut the carrots, cucumber and nori sheet into thin matchsticks, and thinly slice the avocado. Toss the sesame seeds in a small nonstick frying pan over a high heat for 1 minute, or until lightly toasted.

**3** Combine the ginger, mirin, soy sauce, caster sugar, sesame oil and wasabi paste in a small bowl. Combine the rice, tuna, carrots, cucumber, avocado and pea shoots in a large bowl. Transfer to a serving plate and drizzle with the mirin dressing, then sprinkle with the nori and sesame seeds to serve.

SmartPoints values per serving 9
SmartPoints values per recipe 37

# Rare roast beef with chickpea salad

*Serves 4*

*Prep time*
10 minutes

Chickpeas make a great addition to a summery salad. This one uses yogurt as a simple dressing.

## Ingredients

2 large tomatoes, thinly sliced
¼ small red onion, thinly sliced
300g cooked rare roast beef, thinly sliced
1 cucumber, sliced into ribbons
350g tinned chickpeas, drained and rinsed
160g 0% fat natural Greek yogurt

1 Arrange the tomatoes, beef and red onion on serving plates.

2 Top with the cucumber, chickpeas and a dollop of yogurt. Season to taste and serve immediately.

**SmartPoints** values per serving 4
**SmartPoints** values per recipe 16

# Tandoori salmon with lime pickle yogurt

A delicious twist on salmon fillets, this recipe uses ready-made tandoori paste to spice things up.

**Serves 4**

**Prep time**
4 minutes

**Cook time**
6 minutes

## Ingredients

4 x 120g skinless salmon fillets
2 tablespoons tandoori paste (ensure gluten free)
Calorie controlled cooking spray
2 x 250g packs microwaveable brown rice
1 tablespoon lime pickle (ensure gluten free)
120g 0% fat natural Greek yogurt
3 spring onions, trimmed and thinly sliced
Large handful of fresh coriander, roughly chopped
80g young leaf spinach

1 Put the salmon and the tandoori paste in a small bowl and gently mix to coat the salmon. Mist a large nonstick frying pan with the cooking spray and cook the salmon over a medium heat for 3 minutes on each side, or until cooked to your liking.

2 Meanwhile, cook the rice according to pack instructions. Put the lime pickle and the yogurt in a small bowl and stir well to combine.

3 Put the rice, spring onions and coriander in a medium bowl and stir to combine. Serve the salmon with the rice, spinach and lime pickle yogurt on the side.

**SmartPoints** values per serving 12
**SmartPoints** values per recipe 46

## Cook's tip

To make this No Count, use wholewheat pasta and cottage cheese, instead of ricotta.

**15 MINUTES & UNDER**

# Courgette, lemon & ricotta linguine

An easy pasta dish that's full of zingy, fresh flavours. The ricotta helps create a creamy sauce.

**Serves 4**

**Prep time**
6 minutes

**Cook time**
7 minutes

### Ingredients
500g fresh linguine pasta
Calorie controlled
cooking spray
2 garlic cloves, thinly sliced
1 red chilli, deseeded and
finely chopped
2 courgettes,
coarsely grated
Grated zest and juice
of 1 lemon
170g ricotta cheese,
broken up
Large handful of fresh mint,
coarsely chopped

1 Fill and boil the kettle. Pour the boiling water into a large saucepan and return to the boil over a high heat. Add the pasta and cook according to pack instructions. Drain, reserving 120ml of the cooking liquid, then return the pasta to the pan.

2 Meanwhile, mist a large nonstick frying pan with the cooking spray. Cook the garlic and chilli over a medium heat, stirring, for 1 minute or until fragrant. Add the courgettes and cook, stirring, for 2-3 minutes. Season to taste.

3 Add the lemon zest and juice, ricotta, mint, courgette mixture and the reserved cooking liquid to the pasta; toss to combine, then serve.

**SmartPoints** values per serving 12
**SmartPoints** values per recipe 49

# Chicken & ramen noodle soup

**Serves 4**

**Prep time**
4 minutes

**Cook time**
10 minutes

Quick cook noodles make this speedy to prepare. Use Asian mushrooms, if you can find them.

## Ingredients
4 eggs
170g dried egg noodles
1 chicken stock cube
1 tablespoon soy sauce
500g mixed mushrooms, sliced if large
300g cooked skinless chicken breast, sliced
80g young leaf spinach

1 Boil the eggs in a pan of boiling water for 5 minutes. Drain and cool under running cold water, then peel and cut in half. This can be done ahead of time, if you like. Fill and boil the kettle.

2 While the eggs are cooking, cook the noodles according to pack instructions, then drain and divide among 4 serving bowls. In a large jug, mix 1.5 litres boiling water from the kettle with the stock cube and soy sauce. Top the noodles with the mushrooms, then pour over the stock.

3 Divide the chicken, spinach and boiled eggs among the serving bowls and serve immediately.

**SmartPoints** values per serving 7
**SmartPoints** values per recipe 28

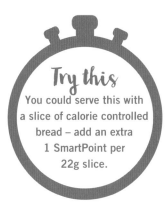

**Try this**
You could serve this with a slice of calorie controlled bread – add an extra 1 SmartPoint per 22g slice.

## 15 MINUTES & UNDER

# Quick seafood stew

*Serves 4*

**Prep time**
4 minutes

**Cook time**
11 minutes

### Ingredients
Calorie controlled cooking spray
1 onion, finely chopped
2 red peppers, deseeded and thinly sliced
120g chorizo, diced
2 teaspoons mild paprika
¼ teaspoon dried chilli flakes
400g tin chopped tomatoes
600g mixed seafood and cubed fish
50g mixed olives, halved
Handful of fresh flat-leaf parsley, torn
Fresh rocket, to serve

Use a ready-prepared fish pie mix or seafood mix from the supermarket to make this really speedy.

1 Mist a deep nonstick frying pan with the cooking spray and put over a medium-high heat. Add the onion, peppers and chorizo, stirring, for 2 minutes or until the onion and peppers have softened. Add the paprika and chilli flakes, and stir for 1 minute or until the paprika is fragrant.

2 Add the tomatoes, along with 125ml water, and bring to the boil. Add the seafood and simmer gently, stirring occasionally for 2 minutes, then add the fish and cook for another 4-6 minutes, or until the seafood and fish are cooked through.

3 Serve the stew topped with olives, parsley and rocket.

**SmartPoints** values per serving 7
**SmartPoints** values per recipe 26

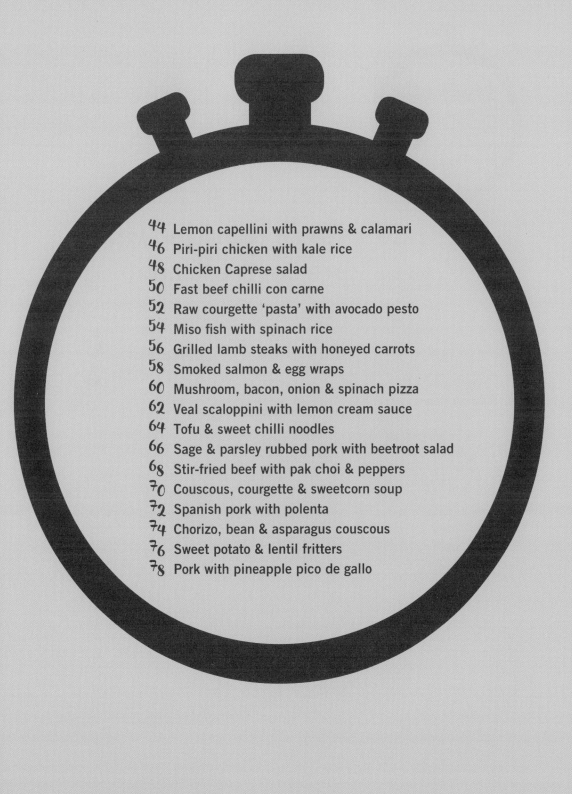

**Inside info**
Capellini pasta (also called 'angel hair') is thinner and quicker to cook than spaghetti.

**20 MINUTES & UNDER**

# Lemon capellini with prawns & calamari

Serves 4

Prep time
7 minutes

Cook time
8 minutes

A squeeze of lemon and lots of parsley bring out the flavour of the seafood in this delicous pasta dish.

### Ingredients
2 garlic cloves, crushed
300g raw prawns, peeled
250g dried capellini pasta
Calorie controlled cooking spray
300g raw squid rings
1 teaspoon dried chilli flakes
Zest and juice of 1 lemon, plus lemon wedges, to serve
2 tablespoons chopped fresh flat-leaf parsley

1 Put the garlic in a bowl, add the prawns and mix well. Cover with foil and set aside.

2 Fill and boil the kettle. Pour boiling water into a large saucepan and return to the boil over a high heat. Add the pasta to the boiling water and cook, following pack instructions, or until al dente. Drain, reserving 125ml of the cooking water.

3 Meanwhile, mist a large nonstick frying pan with cooking spray. Add the prawns and garlic, squid rings and chilli, then cook, stirring, for 3-4 minutes over a high heat or until the seafood is just cooked through. Add the lemon zest and toss to combine, then season to taste.

4 Add the lemon juice, pasta and reserved cooking liquid to the seafood mixture and toss to combine. Sprinkle with the parsley, then serve with the lemon wedges.

**SmartPoints** values per serving 7
**SmartPoints** values per recipe 29

**Cook's tip**

This is a great way to use up extra cooked rice. To make this No Count, use brown rice.

*Serves 4*

*Prep time*
10 minutes

*Cook time*
10 minutes

# Piri-piri chicken with kale rice

Spicy chicken breast is served alongside a colourful, fresh-tasting veggie and rice mix.

## Ingredients

1 teaspoon dried oregano

1 teaspoon sweet paprika

½ teaspoon dried chilli flakes

Grated zest and juice of ½ lemon, plus extra lemon wedges to serve

2 x 250g skinless chicken breasts

Calorie controlled cooking spray

100g ready-chopped curly leaf kale

1 large courgette, coarsely grated

340g cooked basmati rice

250g cherry tomatoes, halved

1 Mix the oregano, paprika, chilli and lemon zest in a small bowl. Cut each chicken breast horizontally into two thin fillets. Sprinkle the spice mixture over the chicken pieces.

2 Mist a large nonstick frying pan with the cooking spray, add the chicken and cook for 2-3 minutes over a medium heat, or until cooked through.

3 Meanwhile mist a second large nonstick frying pan with the cooking spray. Add the kale and courgette and cook over a medium heat, stirring, for 2 minutes or until just tender. Add the cooked rice and cook, stirring, for 2 minutes or until heated through. Remove from the heat.

4 Stir in the tomatoes and lemon juice and season to taste. Serve the chicken with the kale rice and lemon wedges.

**SmartPoints** values per serving 5
**SmartPoints** values per recipe 18

# Chicken Caprese salad

**Serves 4**

Adding chicken and bread to this popular tomato and mozzarella salad makes it a meal in itself.

**Prep time**
8 minutes

**Cook time**
12 minutes

### Ingredients
Calorie controlled
cooking spray
1 teaspoon olive oil
600g skinless
chicken breasts
4 x 35g slices crusty
white bread
2 tablespoons green pesto
1 tablespoon lemon juice
2 large tomatoes, sliced
125g mozzarella, sliced

1 Mist a large nonstick frying pan with the cooking spray and put over a medium heat. Add the whole chicken breasts and cook, turning often, for 10-12 minutes or until cooked through. Transfer the chicken breasts to a plate.

2 Meanwhile, toast the bread until golden. Set aside for 2 minutes to cool and then tear into bite-size pieces. Combine the pesto and lemon juice in a small bowl.

3 Slice the chicken thickly. Arrange the tomatoes and mozzarella on plates and top with the chicken and bread pieces. Drizzle with the pesto dressing to serve.

**SmartPoints** values per serving 8
**SmartPoints** values per recipe 33

# Fast beef chilli con carne

Chilli con carne doesn't have to take hours – this version uses sirloin steak and cooks in minutes.

**Serves 4**

**Prep time**
8 minutes

**Cook time**
12 minutes

## Ingredients

160g quick cook
basmati rice
2 x 200g lean sirloin
steaks, fat trimmed and
thinly sliced
1 teaspoon ground cumin
Pinch dried chilli flakes
Calorie controlled
cooking spray
2 tomatoes, chopped
1 green pepper, deseeded
and chopped
400g tin red kidney beans,
drained and rinsed
Small handful of chopped
fresh coriander leaves, plus
extra sprigs to garnish
1 small avocado, peeled,
stone removed and diced

1 Cook the rice according to the pack instructions.

2 Meanwhile, put the steak, cumin and chilli in a medium bowl and mix to coat the steak. Mist a large nonstick frying pan with the cooking spray and put on a medium-high heat. Add the steak and cook, stirring, for 4 minutes or until just browned. Transfer the steak to a plate.

3 Add the tomatoes and green pepper to the same pan and cook, stirring, for 4 minutes or until softened. Return the steak to the pan with the kidney beans and and cook, stirring, for 1 minute or until heated through. Season to taste, and stir in the chopped coriander.

4 Serve the chilli con carne topped with the avocado and extra coriander, with the rice on the side.

**SmartPoints** values per serving 10
**SmartPoints** values per recipe 41

# Raw courgette 'pasta' with avocado pesto

*Serves 4*

*Prep time*
15 minutes

A healthy, no-cook courgetti dish with an avocado and pesto sauce, topped with cottage cheese.

## Ingredients
4 large courgettes
½ avocado, peeled and stone removed
2 tablespoons green pesto
2 tablespoons lemon juice
150g cherry tomatoes, quartered
200g reduced-fat cottage cheese
120g young leaf spinach
4 x 35g slices wholegrain bread
Lemon wedges, to serve

1 Using a spiraliser or julienne peeler, slice the courgettes into spaghetti-like strips.

2 Mash the avocado, pesto and lemon juice in a medium bowl until smooth. Add the courgette spaghetti and tomatoes, and mix carefully. Put the mixture onto 4 plates, top with the cottage cheese and season to taste. Serve with the spinach, bread and lemon wedges.

**SmartPoints** values per serving 5
**SmartPoints** values per recipe 21

# Miso fish with spinach rice

*Serves 4*

*Prep time*
5 minutes

*Cook time*
15 minutes

This Asian-inspired dish is so simple to make. The miso paste adds a delicious savoury note to the fish.

## Ingredients
75g miso paste
1 tablespoon soy sauce
2 tablespoons mirin
1 tablespoon caster sugar
2 teaspoons sesame oil
4 x 150g firm white
fish fillets
2 x 250g packs
microwaveable brown rice
250g frozen spinach
200g shelled soya beans
200g Tenderstem broccoli
90g pickled ginger

1 Put a large foil-lined baking tray under the grill. Preheat the grill to high. Combine the miso, soy sauce, mirin, sugar and sesame oil in a medium bowl. Add the fish and turn to coat.

2 Carefully remove the hot baking tray from under the grill and arrange the fish on the tray. Grill for 6-8 minutes on one side or until the fish is just cooked through (be careful that the coating on the fish doesn't burn).

3 Meanwhile, fill and boil the kettle. Pour the boiling water into a large saucepan, add the broccoli and return to the boil over a high heat for 3-5 minutes. Microwave the rice, spinach and soya beans according to pack instructions. Combine the rice, spinach and soya beans in a large bowl. Serve the fish with the spinach rice, broccoli and pickled ginger.

**SmartPoints** values per serving 12
**SmartPoints** values per recipe 48

# Grilled lamb steaks with honeyed carrots

*Serves 4*

*Prep time*
6 minutes

*Cook time*
10 minutes

Ready-made pesto makes an instant sauce for the lamb, served with baby potatoes and carrots.

## Ingredients
500g baby potatoes, halved
Calorie controlled cooking spray
4 x 120g lean lamb steaks
2 teaspoons ground coriander
2 teaspoons garlic-infused olive oil
300g baby topped carrots
3 teaspoons clear honey
2 tablespoons green pesto

1 Put a large griddle pan over a high heat to preheat. Put the potatoes in a microwave-proof dish. Cover and cook on high for 8-10 minutes, or until tender.

2 Meanwhile, mist the lamb with the cooking spray and sprinkle with the coriander. Put the steaks in the griddle pan and cook for 3-4 minutes each side or until cooked to your liking. Transfer the steaks to a plate, cover with foil and set aside to rest for 2 minutes.

3 Meanwhile, heat the garlic-infused oil in a large nonstick frying pan over a medium heat. Add the carrots and cook, turning occasionally, for 5-6 minutes or until tender. Add the honey and toss to coat.

4 Top the lamb with the pesto and serve with the carrots and potatoes.

**SmartPoints** values per serving 12
**SmartPoints** values per recipe 46

# Smoked salmon & egg wraps

**Serves 4**

**Prep time**
11 minutes

**Cook time**
4 minutes

Perfect for an easy lunch-on-the-go, these wraps are filled with a tasty omelette and salmon combo.

## Ingredients

8 eggs
Calorie controlled cooking spray
4 Weight Watchers Wraps
60g young leaf spinach
200g smoked salmon
4 spring onions, shredded
6 radishes, cut into matchsticks

1 Whisk the eggs and 1 tablespoon of water in a large jug until combined. Season to taste.

2 Mist a large frying pan with the cooking spray and preheat over a medium-high heat. Add a quarter of the egg mixture and swirl to coat the pan. Cook for 1 minute or until just set. Transfer the omelette to a plate. Repeat with the remaining egg mixture to make 3 more omelettes.

3 Top each wrap with an omelette and divide the spinach, salmon, spring onions and radishes between them. Roll each wrap carefully to enclose the filling. Cut each roll in half and serve.

**SmartPoints** values per serving 9
**SmartPoints** values per recipe 34

**Inside info**

Try this using gluten free pitta as a base for an extra 1 Smartpoint per serving.

GF

*Serves 4*

**Prep time**
7 minutes

**Cook time**
13 minutes

### Ingredients
2 x 65g flatbreads
Calorie controlled cooking spray
3 slices Weight Watchers Unsmoked Extra Trimmed Back Bacon, chopped
1 small onion, chopped
300g chestnut mushrooms, sliced
6 tablespoons tomato purée
150g young leaf spinach
160g reduced-fat cottage cheese

## 20 MINUTES & UNDER

# Mushroom, bacon, onion & spinach pizza

Easier, quicker and healthier than a takeaway, this pizza uses a ready-made flatbread for a base.

1 Preheat the oven to 200°C, fan 180°C, gas mark 6. Line 2 baking trays with baking paper. Put the bread on trays.

2 Meanwhile, mist a large nonstick frying pan with the cooking spray. Cook the bacon, onion and mushrooms over a medium-high heat, stirring, for 3 minutes.

3 Spread the flatbreads with the tomato purée. Set aside a large handful of the spinach. Top the flatbreads with the remaining spinach and cottage cheese. Bake for 10 minutes or until the bases are golden and crisp. Cut the pizzas in half and serve topped with the reserved spinach.

**SmartPoints** values per serving 5
**SmartPoints** values per recipe 21

**Try this**
You could serve this with sourdough bread – add an extra 2 SmartPoints per 35g slice.

## 20 MINUTES & UNDER

# Veal scaloppini with lemon cream sauce

This classic Italian veal dish is served with a tasty fennel, celery and apple salad.

**Serves 4**

**Prep time**
12 minutes

**Cook time**
8 minutes

### Ingredients
1 fennel bulb, thinly sliced
4 celery sticks, cut into matchsticks
4 radishes, thinly sliced
1 green apple, cored and cut into matchsticks
2 tablespoons chopped fresh flat-leaf parsley, plus extra sprigs to garnish
2 tablespoons lemon juice
2 teaspoons olive oil
Calorie controlled cooking spray
4 x 125g veal escalopes
2 teaspoons capers, chopped
2 garlic cloves, crushed
125ml chicken stock, made with ½ cube (ensure gluten free)
80ml fat-reduced crème fraîche

1 Combine the fennel, celery, radishes, apple, half the chopped parsley, half the lemon juice and the olive oil in a large bowl.

2 Mist a large nonstick frying pan with the cooking spray and put over a high heat. Add the veal escalopes and cook for 1–2 minutes on each side or until cooked to your liking. Transfer to a plate, cover with foil and set aside to rest for 2 minutes.

3 While the veal is resting, put the capers and garlic in the pan and cook, stirring, for 30 seconds or until fragrant. Add the stock and remaining lemon juice and bring to the boil. Reduce the heat and simmer until reduced by half. Add the crème fraîche and cook for 2 minutes or until slightly thickened. Remove from the heat and stir in the remaining chopped parsley.

4 Put the veal onto serving plates and drizzle with the sauce, then top with the extra parsley sprigs and serve with the fennel salad.

**SmartPoints** values per serving 3
**SmartPoints** values per recipe 11

**Try this**

You could make this with 400g cooked prawns instead of the tofu – the SmartPoints will be the same.

**20 MINUTES & UNDER**

# Tofu & sweet chilli noodles

Use your favourite ready-prepared stir-fry vegetable mix in this easy Asian-inspired noodle dish.

*Serves 4*

*Prep time*
3 minutes

*Cook time*
13 minutes

*Ingredients*
3 x 150g pack wok-ready noodles
Calorie controlled cooking spray
1 onion, cut into wedges
300g firm tofu, cut into 2cm cubes
2 garlic cloves, crushed
60ml sweet chilli sauce
80ml Soy with Garlic & Ginger Stir-fry Sauce
325g pack stir-fry vegetable mix

1 Fill and boil the kettle. Put the noodles in a large heatproof bowl. Cover with boiling water and set aside for 3 minutes to soften. Drain the noodles.

2 Meanwhile, heat a wok over a high heat. Mist it with the cooking spray, then add the onion and stir-fry for 2–3 minutes or until softened. Add the tofu and garlic and stir-fry for 5 minutes or until the tofu has browned all over (take care not to break up tofu). Transfer the tofu to a plate and set aside.

3 Add the sweet chilli sauce, stir-fry sauce and vegetables to the wok, then stir-fry for about 5 minutes until the vegetables start to soften. Add the noodles and tofu to the wok and stir gently to heat through. Season to taste and serve immediately.

**SmartPoints** values per recipe 10
**SmartPoints** values per recipe 41

### Try this

You could serve this with sourdough bread – add an extra 2 SmartPoints per 35g slice.

## 20 MINUTES & UNDER

# Sage & parsley rubbed pork with beetroot salad

Fresh herbs add lots of extra flavour and colour to this succulent roast pork tenderloin.

*Serves 4*

*Prep time*
8 minutes

*Cook time*
12 minutes

## Ingredients

2 tablespoons chopped fresh flat-leaf parsley
1 tablespoon chopped fresh sage
Grated zest of ½ lemon
600g lean pork tenderloin
Calorie controlled cooking spray
450g pickled baby beetroot
150g sugar snap peas
100g rocket
2 teaspoons olive oil
2 teaspoons balsamic vinegar

1 Preheat the oven to 200°C, fan 180°C, gas mark 6. Line a baking tray with baking paper.

2 Meanwhile, combine the parsley, sage and zest in a small bowl. Mist the pork with the cooking spray. Sprinkle both sides of the pork with the sage mixture. Mist a large nonstick frying pan with the cooking spray and put over a medium-high heat. Add the pork and cook for 1 minute on each side or until browned. Transfer to the prepared baking tray.

3 Roast the pork for 10 minutes or until just cooked through. Transfer it to a plate, cover with foil and set aside to rest for 2 minutes, then slice thinly.

4 Meanwhile, drain and cube the beetroot and thinly slice the peas. Combine the beetroot, peas, rocket and olive oil in a large bowl and season to taste. Top the salad with pork and drizzle with the balsamic vinegar to serve.

**SmartPoints** values per serving 4
**SmartPoints** values per recipe 16

**Try this**

You could serve this with 125g cooked basmati rice for 5 extra SmartPoints per serving.

## 20 MINUTES & UNDER

# Stir-fried beef with pak choi & peppers

Crunchy fresh baby peppers and mangetout make this stir-fry colourful, as well as healthy.

**Serves 4**

**Prep time**
10 minutes

**Cook time**
10 minutes

### Ingredients

Calorie controlled cooking spray
500g lean beef rump steak, fat trimmed, thinly sliced
1 onion, cut into wedges
4 garlic cloves, thinly sliced
2cm-piece fresh ginger, grated,
175g mixed baby peppers, deseeded & sliced
150g mangetout
250g baby pak choi, quartered, cut into 6cm lengths
1 tablespoon soy sauce (ensure gluten free)
1½ tablespoons oyster sauce (ensure gluten free)
Small handful of fresh coriander

1 Mist a wok with the cooking spray and put over a high heat for 20 seconds. Add the beef and stir-fry, in two batches, for 2 minutes or until browned. Transfer to a plate.

2 Mist the wok with the cooking spray again, add the onion and stir-fry for 2 minutes or until lightly browned. Add the garlic and ginger, then stir-fry for 30 seconds or until fragrant. Add the peppers and mangetout and stir-fry for 2 minutes or until almost tender. Add the pak choi and stir-fry for another 1–2 minutes or until just tender.

3 Return the beef to the wok with the soy and oyster sauces, and cook, stirring, until heated through. Serve topped with the coriander.

**SmartPoints** values per serving 3
**SmartPoints** values per recipe 12

# Couscous, courgette & sweetcorn soup

A Middle Eastern-inspired soup that's flavoured with harissa and topped with fresh coriander.

Serves 4

Prep time
10 minutes

Cook time
10 minutes

## Ingredients

2 teaspoons olive oil
1 onion, finely chopped
3 celery sticks, finely chopped
2 garlic cloves, crushed
240g frozen sweetcorn
200g green beans chopped
1 litre vegetable stock, made with 2 stock cubes
1 large courgette, chopped
100g wholemeal couscous
1 tablespoon harissa paste
Small handful of fresh coriander, chopped

1 Heat the oil in a large pan over a medium heat. Add the onion and celery, and cook for 5 minutes or until softened. Add the crushed garlic and cook, stirring, for 30 seconds or until fragrant.

2 Add the corn, beans and stock, and bring to the boil. Reduce the heat and simmer, uncovered for 2 minutes. Add the courgette and couscous and simmer, uncovered for 2-3 minutes or until the couscous is tender. Season to taste.

3 Serve the soup with the harissa paste and fresh coriander sprinkled over the top.

**SmartPoints** values per serving 5
**SmartPoints** values per recipe 21

# Spanish pork with polenta

**Serves 4**

**Prep time**
10 minutes

**Cook time**
10 minutes

Tender pork steaks are served with a lemon and caper sauce, with polenta on the side.

## Ingredients

1 litre chicken stock, made with 2 cubes (ensure gluten free)
170g polenta
Calorie controlled cooking spray
4 x 100g lean pork escalopes
1 teaspoon smoked paprika
1 tablespoon capers, rinsed and drained
2 garlic cloves, crushed
1 tablespoon Dijon mustard
Juice of 1 large lemon, plus extra lemon wedges to serve
30g pitted green olives, thinly sliced
350g broccoli, cut into florets
Handful of fresh flat-leaf parsley, chopped

1 Fill and boil the kettle. Mix 875ml of the stock with 125ml boiling water in a medium saucepan and bring to the boil over a high heat. Add the polenta in a thin, steady stream and cook, stirring, for 5 minutes until soft and creamy.

2 Meanwhile, mist a medium nonstick frying pan with cooking spray and heat over medium-high heat. Sprinkle the pork with the paprika and season to taste. Cook the pork for 2 minutes on each side or until browned. Transfer to a plate.

3 Add the capers and garlic to the pan and cook for 1 minute or until fragrant. Add the mustard, lemon juice, olives and remaining stock, and bring to the boil. Reduce the heat and simmer, uncovered, for 2 minutes or until the sauce has thickened slightly. Return the pork and any juices to the pan and turn to coat. Cover and set aside to rest for 2 minutes.

4 Put the broccoli in a microwave-proof bowl with 2 tablespoons water and cook on high for 2 minutes. Serve the pork and sauce with the polenta and broccoli, garnished with parsley and with the lemon wedges on the side.

**SmartPoints** values per serving 8
**SmartPoints** values per recipe 31

## Cook's tip

Pomegranate molasses is a thick syrup that gives savoury dishes a hint of tangy fruitiness.

**Serves 4**

**Prep time**
7 minutes
**Cook time**
11 minutes

### Ingredients

120g diced chorizo
160g couscous
2 bunches asparagus,
cut into 3cm lengths
2 x 400g tins haricot
beans, rinsed and drained
80g red cabbage, shredded
Small handful of fresh
mint, torn
Small handful of fresh
flat-leaf parsley, torn
1 tablespoon pomegranate
molasses
1½ tablespoons
lemon juice, plus extra
lemon wedges, to serve

**20 MINUTES & UNDER**

# Chorizo, bean & asparagus couscous

A delicious Mediterranean-style dish finished off with fresh herbs and pomegranate molasses.

1  Fill and boil the kettle. Put a large nonstick frying pan over a medium-high heat. Add the chorizo and cook, stirring, for 6-7 minutes.

2  Meanwhile, put the couscous in a large heatproof bowl. Add 160ml of boiling water. Stir, cover and set aside for 5 minutes or until the liquid has been absorbed. Fluff up the couscous with a fork to separate the grains.

3  Meanwhile, boil, steam or microwave the asparagus until just tender, then drain.

4  Add the chorizo, asparagus, beans, cabbage, mint, parsley, pomegranate molasses and lemon juice to the couscous and toss to combine. Season to taste and serve with the lemon wedges on the side.

**SmartPoints** values per serving 11
**SmartPoints** values per recipe 45

# Sweet potato & lentil fritters

*Serves 4*

*Prep time*
12 minutes

*Cook time*
8 minutes

This Middle Eastern-inspired dish gets a flavour boost from tahini, a sesame seed paste.

### Ingredients

75g self-raising flour
2 eggs
60ml skimmed milk
300g sweet potato,
coarsely grated
410g tin green lentils,
rinsed and drained
4 spring onions,
thinly sliced
Handful of fresh mint,
finely chopped
Calorie controlled
cooking spray
120g 0% fat natural yogurt
2 teaspoons tahini
1 tablespoon lemon juice
Garden salad, to serve

1 Sift the flour into a large bowl and make a well in the centre. Whisk the eggs and milk in a small jug until combined. Pour the egg mixture into the well in the flour and whisk until smooth. Add the grated sweet potato, the lentils, spring onions and three-quarters of the mint. Season to taste and stir to combine.

2 Mist a large nonstick frying pan with the cooking spray and put on a medium-high heat. Spoon four 60ml portions of sweet-potato mixture into the pan. Cook the fritters for 2 minutes on each side or until cooked through. Re-mist the pan with the cooking spray and make 4 more fritters.

3 Meanwhile, combine the yogurt, tahini, lemon juice and remaining mint in a bowl. Season to taste and serve the fritters with the tahini yogurt. Serve with a garden salad.

**SmartPoints** values per serving 8
**SmartPoints** values per recipe 31

# Pork with pineapple pico de gallo

*Serves 4*

**Prep time**
8 minutes

**Cook time**
12 minutes

Pico de gallo is a fresh salsa made with lime juice that's very popular in Mexican cuisine.

## Ingredients

3 teaspoons olive oil
350g sweet potato, thinly sliced
½ fresh pineapple
½ large avocado
2 tomatoes
¼ small red onion
Small handful of fresh coriander
1 small red chilli, deseeded
Juice of ½ lime
4 x 100g lean pork loin steaks, fat trimmed
1 teaspoon ground cumin
Salad leaves, to serve

1 Heat 1 teaspoon of the oil in a large nonstick frying pan over a medium heat. Add half the sweet potato and cook for 2 minutes each side or until light golden. Transfer to a plate. Cover with foil to keep warm. Repeat with another teaspoon of oil and the remaining sweet potato.

2 Meanwhile, make the pico de gallo. Take the skin off the pineapple, peel the avocado and remove the stone. Chop the pineapple, avocado, tomatoes and onion and put in a medium bowl. Finely chop the coriander and chilli, and add to the bowl along with the lime juice, then toss to combine.

3 Sprinkle the pork with the cumin and season to taste. Heat the remaining oil in the frying pan over a medium heat. Cook the pork for 2 minutes on each side or until just cooked through. Transfer to a plate, cover with foil and set aside to rest for 2 minutes, then serve with the sweet potato, the pico de gallo and salad leaves.

**SmartPoints** values per serving 9
**SmartPoints** values per recipe 37

30 minutes
& under

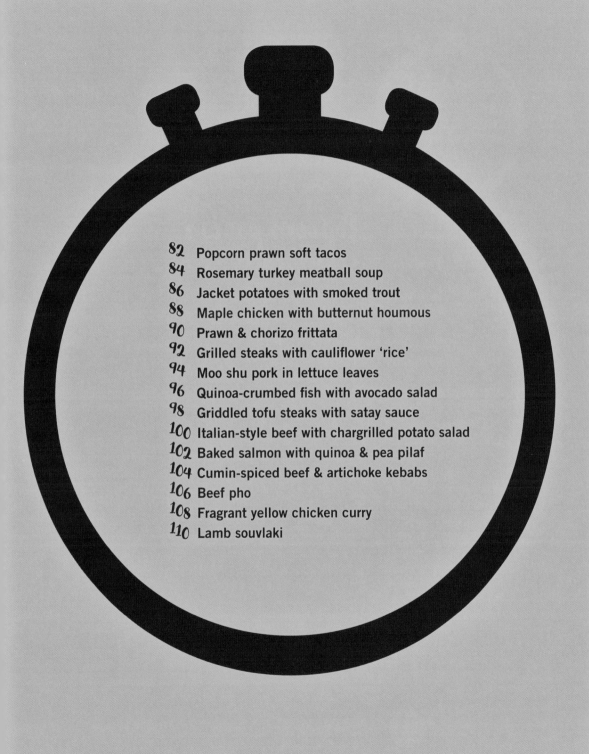

**Cook's tip**

Use a ready-prepared supermarket salad mix, or make your own with grated carrot and shredded cabbage.

**30 MINUTES & UNDER**

# Popcorn prawn soft tacos

This summery take on a Mexican taco features crispy fried prawns and a delicious dressing.

**Serves 4**

**Prep time**
12 minutes

**Cook time**
8 minutes

## Ingredients
1 egg white
25g panko breadcrumbs
400g raw prawns, peeled
1 tablespoon olive oil
2 tablespoons reduced-fat mayonnaise
60ml buttermilk
1 tablespoon lime juice
300g ready-prepared salad mix (see Cook's tip)
100g tinned sweetcorn, drained
8 x 30g mini tortilla wraps
40g rocket
2 tablespoons salsa dip
Lime wedges, to serve

1 Whisk the egg white and 1 tablespoon of water in a bowl. Put the breadcrumbs on a plate. Working with one at a time, dip the prawns in the egg white mixture. Coat in the breadcrumbs and put on a plate.

2 Heat the oil in a large nonstick frying pan over a medium-high heat. Add the prawns and cook, in two batches, for 2 minutes each side or until just cooked through. Transfer to a plate lined with baking paper.

3 Meanwhile, combine the mayonnaise, buttermilk and lime juice in a small bowl and season to taste. Reserve 2 tablespoons of the dressing. Put the salad mix and sweetcorn in a large bowl. Add the remaining dressing and toss gently to combine.

4 Heat the tortilla wraps in the microwave according to pack instructions. Divide half the rocket and two-thirds of the salad and sweetcorn along the centre of the tortillas. Top with the prawns and salsa and drizzle with the reserved dressing. Fold the tortillas to enclose the filling. Serve with the remaining salad and sweetcorn, and the lime wedges.

**SmartPoints** values per serving 11
**SmartPoints** values per recipe 42

**30 MINUTES & UNDER**

*Serves 4*

*Prep time*
10 minutes

*Cook time*
20 minutes

# Rosemary turkey meatball soup

A hearty soup of onion and celery with flavoursome meatballs, topped with rocket and Parmesan.

## Ingredients

Calorie controlled cooking spray
1 onion, finely chopped
2 celery sticks, finely chopped
1.5 litres chicken stock, made with 3 cubes
2 garlic cloves, crushed
165g orzo pasta
500g turkey breast mince
1 tablespoon finely chopped fresh rosemary
Grated zest of ½ lemon
2 teaspoons olive oil
60g rocket
40g Parmesan, grated

1 Mist a large saucepan with cooking spray over a medium heat. Add the onion and celery and cook, stirring, for 3-4 minutes or until softened. Add the stock and half the garlic and bring to the boil. Reduce the heat to a simmer and add the orzo. Cook, uncovered, for 10 minutes or until the pasta is tender.

2 Meanwhile, combine the mince, rosemary, lemon zest and remaining garlic in a bowl, then season to taste. Roll tablespoons of the mixture into walnut-size balls. Heat the olive oil in a large nonstick frying pan over a medium heat. Add the meatballs and cook, turning occasionally, for 5-6 minutes or until browned and cooked through. Add the meatballs to the orzo mixture.

3 Serve the soup topped with the rocket and Parmesan.

**SmartPoints** values per serving 8
**SmartPoints** values per recipe 32

# Jacket potatoes with smoked trout

**Serves 4**

**Prep time**
18 minutes

**Cook time**
12 minutes

Traditional baked potatoes are topped with hot-smoked trout and served with a tomato salsa.

## Ingredients

4 x 180g Desiree potatoes, unpeeled
350g hot-smoked trout
2 tomatoes, chopped
¼ small red onion, finely chopped
1 tablespoon olive oil
Grated zest of ½ lemon
2 teaspoons balsamic vinegar
2 teaspoons creamed horseradish
4 tablespoons fat-reduced sour cream
1 tablespoon fresh chives, chopped
Lemon wedges, to serve

1 Line a microwave-proof plate with a paper towel. Use a fork to prick the potatoes all over. Put the potatoes on the paper towel and microwave on high for 10-12 minutes or until tender. Set aside for 3 minutes or until cool enough to handle.

2 Meanwhile, remove any skin and bones from the trout and coarsely flake the flesh. Set aside. To make the salsa, combine the tomatoes and onion in a small bowl. Mix the olive oil with the lemon zest. Drizzle the tomato and onion with the vinegar and 1 teaspoon of the lemon oil. In a small bowl, combine the horseradish and 2 tablespoons sour cream.

3 Using a sharp knife, cut the tops off each potato. Discard the tops and scoop out the potato flesh, leaving 2cm-thick shells. Mash the potato flesh together with the remaining lemon oil and remaining sour cream in a bowl. Spoon the potato mixture back into the shells.

4 Top the filled potatoes with the flaked trout and horseradish mixture. Sprinkle with the chives and serve with the tomato salsa and lemon wedges.

**SmartPoints** values per serving 10
**SmartPoints** values per recipe 38

# Maple chicken with butternut houmous

*Serves 4*

*Prep time*
15 minutes
*Cook time*
15 minutes

Succulent chicken topped with a sticky maple glaze and served with a butternut and chickpea mash.

## Ingredients

600g butternut squash, peeled and chopped
1 tablespoon tahini (ensure gluten free)
200g tinned chickpeas, drained and rinsed
Juice of ½ orange, plus orange wedges, to serve
1 teaspoon ground cumin
600g skinless chicken breast
1 tablespoon sweet chilli sauce
2 teaspoons sesame oil
2 tablespoons maple syrup
Calorie controlled cooking spray
500g Brussels sprouts, trimmed and halved

1 Put the butternut squash with a little water in a microwave-proof dish, cover loosely and microwave on high for 5 minutes or until tender. Drain, then mash in a large bowl with the tahini, chickpeas, orange juice and cumin. Season to taste and cover to keep warm.

2 Meanwhile, cut each chicken breast horizontally into 2 thin fillets. Put the chicken, chilli sauce, sesame oil and maple syrup in a shallow dish and turn to coat. Mist a large nonstick frying pan and heat over a medium-high heat. Add the chicken and cook for 2-3 minutes on each side or until cooked through. Transfer to a plate. Cover the chicken with foil and set aside to rest for 5 minutes.

3 Meanwhile, wipe out the pan, mist with the cooking spray and put on a high heat. Add the sprouts and cook for 3-4 minutes or until tender. Drizzle the chicken with the pan juices and serve with the butternut houmous, sprouts and orange wedges.

**SmartPoints** values per serving 7
**SmartPoints** values per recipe 27

**Try this**
You could serve this with a slice of ciabatta on the side – add an extra 3 SmartPoints per 35g slice.

**30 MINUTES & UNDER**

# Prawn & chorizo frittata

This delicious all-in-one egg dish is full of flavour and great for the whole family.

*Serves 4*

*Prep time*
9 minutes

*Cook time*
21 minutes

## Ingredients

120g chorizo, thinly sliced
Calorie controlled cooking spray
200g raw prawns, peeled
1 red onion, finely chopped
1 red pepper, deseeded and finely chopped
1 garlic clove, crushed
120g frozen peas
4 whole eggs, plus
4 egg whites
1 baby fennel bulb, thinly sliced
100g rocket
Pared zest of 1 lemon, plus
1 tablespoon lemon juice

1 Heat a 15cm nonstick frying pan over a medium heat. Add the chorizo and cook, stirring, for 2 minutes. Transfer to a plate lined with a paper towel.

2 Mist the same frying pan with the cooking spray, add the prawns and cook, stirring, for 2-3 minutes or until just cooked through. Transfer to the plate with the chorizo.

3 Re-mist the same pan with cooking spray, add the onion, pepper and garlic cook, stirring, for 5 minutes or until softened. Add the peas and cook for 1 more minute. Return the chorizo and prawns to the pan and spread to distribute.

4 Meanwhile, preheat the grill to high. Whisk the eggs and egg whites in a large bowl and season to taste. Pour the egg mixture into the pan. Cook on the hob for 5 minutes or until the base and sides are just set, then put the pan under a grill and cook for another 4-5 minutes or until puffed and golden.

5 Meanwhile, combine the fennel, rocket, lemon zest and juice in a bowl. Season to taste. Cut the frittata into wedges and serve with the fennel salad.

**SmartPoints** values per serving 7
**SmartPoints** values per recipe 27

**Inside info**

Sumac is a tangy spice that is often used in Mediterranean and Middle Eastern cooking.

**30 MINUTES & UNDER**

Serves 4

Prep time
16 minutes

Cook time
14 minutes

# Grilled steaks with cauliflower 'rice'

The cauliflower 'rice' with peas makes a simple but delicious side dish for sirloin steak.

## Ingredients

Calorie controlled cooking spray
4 x 150g lean sirloin steaks, fat trimmed
1 teaspoon fresh thyme
4 tomatoes, halved
200g young leaf spinach
½ cauliflower, roughly chopped
120g frozen peas
2 tablespoons chopped fresh flat-leaf parsley, plus extra sprigs to garnish
2 teaspoons sumac

1 Mist a griddle pan with cooking spray and preheat over a high heat. Sprinkle the steaks with thyme and season to taste. Put the steaks into the pan and cook for 2–3 minutes each side or until cooked to your liking. Transfer to a plate. Cover the meat with foil and set aside to rest for 5 minutes.

2 Meanwhile, mist the tomatoes with cooking spray and season to taste. Cook for 2 minutes each side or until slightly softened. Transfer to a plate and cover to keep warm. Microwave the spinach in a covered microwave-proof dish on high for 2 minutes.

3 Pulse the cauliflower in a food processor until crumbs form. Mist a large nonstick frying pan with cooking spray and put over a high heat. Add the cauliflower and cook for 3 minutes or until tender. Add the peas and cook for 1 more minute or until heated through.

4 Add the parsley and sumac to the cauliflower mixture and stir to combine. Top the cauliflower 'rice' with extra parsley and sprigs and serve with the steaks, spinach and tomatoes.

**SmartPoints** values per serving 6
**SmartPoints** values per recipe 25

**Try this**
You could serve this with jasmine rice on the side – add an extra 4 SmartPoints per 85g serving.

**30 MINUTES & UNDER**

*Serves 4*

*Prep time*
20 minutes

*Cook time*
10 minutes

# Moo shu pork in lettuce leaves

Stir-fried pork with ginger, mushrooms and vegetables is served in iceberg lettuce cups.

## Ingredients

2 teaspoons cornflour
2 tablespoons soy sauce
500g lean pork fillet, fat trimmed, thinly sliced
Calorie controlled cooking spray
2cm-piece fresh ginger, peeled and finely grated
100g shiitake mushrooms, sliced
1 red pepper, deseeded and thinly sliced
1 large carrot, peeled and cut into matchsticks
¼ white cabbage, finely shredded
1 tablespoon hoisin sauce (ensure gluten free)
8 iceberg lettuce leaves
1 spring onion, thinly sliced

1 Combine the cornflour and 1 tablespoon soy sauce in a large dish. Add the pork and mix to coat.

2 Heat a wok over a high heat. Mist with cooking spray and heat for 20 seconds. Add the pork and stir-fry in two batches, for 2 minutes each or until browned. Transfer to a plate.

3 Reheat the wok over a high heat. Mist with cooking spray and heat for 20 seconds. Add the ginger and stir-fry for 30 seconds or until fragrant. Add the mushrooms, pepper and carrot and stir-fry for 2–3 minutes or until almost tender. Add the cabbage and stir-fry for 1 minute or until just wilted.

4 Return the pork to the wok with the hoisin and remaining soy sauce and stir-fry until heated through. Fill the lettuce leaves with the pork mixture and sprinkle with the spring onion to serve.

**SmartPoints** values per serving 5
**SmartPoints** values per recipe 19

# Quinoa-crumbed fish with avocado salad

**Serves 4**

**Prep time**
14 minutes

**Cook time**
16 minutes

Use your favourite white fish for this dish, which is served with a fresh salad and new potatoes.

## Ingredients
35g plain flour
1 egg
1 tablespoon skimmed milk
65g quinoa
Grated zest of ½ lemon
Handful of mixed fresh herbs (such as parsley and chives), chopped
4 x 125g white fish fillets
Calorie controlled cooking spray
300g new potatoes, halved if large
2 bunches asparagus, trimmed
400g mixed cherry tomatoes, halved
½ avocado, peeled, stone removed and chopped
2 teaspoon white balsamic vinegar

1 Put the flour on a plate. Whisk the egg and milk in a shallow bowl. Combine the quinoa, lemon zest and half the herbs on a plate. Working with one piece of fish at a time, coat the fillets in the flour first, then in the egg mixture and finally in the quinoa mixture. Put the fish onto a plate.

2 Mist a large nonstick frying pan with cooking spray over a medium heat. Add the fish and cook for 2–3 minutes each side or until golden and just cooked through.

3 Meanwhile, cook the potatoes in a pan of boiling water for 10 minutes, or until tender. Drain and keep warm. Boil, steam or microwave the asparagus until tender. Drain, refresh under cold water and drain again.

4 Combine the asparagus, tomatoes, avocado, vinegar and remaining herbs in a large bowl. Serve the fish with the salad and new potatoes.

**SmartPoints** values per serving 7
**SmartPoints** values per recipe 26

# Griddled tofu steaks with satay sauce

Serves 4

Prep time
16 minutes

Cook time
14 minutes

The spicy peanut sauce adds lots of flavour to marinated tofu in this Asian-inspired recipe.

## Ingredients

2cm-piece fresh ginger, peeled and finely grated
60ml soy sauce
400g firm tofu, cut into 1cm slices
2 tablespoons crunchy peanut butter
½ teaspoon curry powder
1 tablespoon mirin
1 tablespoon lemon juice
125ml reduced-fat coconut milk
Calorie controlled cooking spray
2 x 250g packs microwaveable basmati rice
200g mangetout
300g Swiss chard, cut into 6cm lengths
300g baby pak choi, cut into 6cm lengths

1 Combine the ginger and 2 tablespoons of soy sauce in a large shallow dish. Arrange the tofu, in a single layer, over the soy mixture and carefully turn to coat. Set aside for 10 minutes.

2 Meanwhile, combine the peanut butter, curry powder, mirin, lemon juice, coconut milk and remaining soy sauce in a small saucepan. Bring to the boil over a medium-high heat. Reduce the heat and simmer, uncovered, for 2–3 minutes or until thickened. Cover to keep warm.

3 Mist a griddle pan with cooking spray and preheat over a medium-high heat. Drain and discard the marinade from the tofu and cook the tofu for 2–3 minutes each side or until heated through.

4 Meanwhile, cook the rice according to pack instructions and boil, steam or microwave the mangetout, Swiss chard and pak choi until just tender. Drain and serve the tofu topped with the satay sauce, alongside the steamed greens and rice.

**SmartPoints** values per serving 11
**SmartPoints** values per recipe 45

# Italian-style beef with chargrilled potato salad

Tender beef steak is flavoured with herbs and spices and served with a zesty salsa verde.

Serves 4

Prep time
12 minutes

Cook time
8 minutes

## Ingredients

Calorie controlled cooking spray
1 tablespoon chopped fresh rosemary
2 teaspoons smoked paprika
2 teaspoons fennel seeds
1 teaspoon cumin seeds
500g piece lean beef skirt, fat trimmed
400g Desiree potatoes
Handful of fresh flat-leaf parsley, finely chopped
Handful of fresh basil, finely chopped
2 teaspoons capers, drained and finely chopped
1 garlic clove, crushed
Juice of ½ lemon, plus lemon wedges, to serve
1 tablespoon olive oil
150g rocket

1 Mist a griddle pan with cooking spray and preheat over a medium-high heat. Combine the rosemary, paprika, fennel seeds and cumin seeds in a small bowl. Sprinkle the mix over the beef and season to taste. Put the meat on a plate, cover and set aside for 10 minutes.

2 Meanwhile, thinly slice the potatoes and griddle them for 2 minutes on each side or until tender. Transfer to a plate and cover to keep warm.

3 Re-mist the griddle pan with cooking spray, add the beef and cook for 2-3 minutes each side or until cooked to your liking. Transfer to a plate. Cover the meat with foil and set aside to rest for 5 minutes before slicing thinly.

4 Meanwhile, combine the parsley, basil, capers, garlic, lemon juice and oil in a small bowl. Season the salsa verde to taste.

5 Combine the potato and rocket in a large bowl. Serve the beef with the salsa verde, potato salad and lemon wedges.

**SmartPoints** values per serving 7
**SmartPoints** values per recipe 27

# Baked salmon with quinoa & pea pilaf

Baking the salmon and tomatoes together helps make this delicious recipe fuss-free.

**Serves 4**

**Prep time**
12 minutes

**Cook time**
18 minutes

### Ingredients

Calorie controlled
cooking spray
1 white onion,
finely chopped
2 garlic cloves, crushed
160g quinoa, rinsed
and drained
1 bunch asparagus,
trimmed and sliced
diagonally
150g sugar snap
peas, sliced
120g frozen peas
4 x 100g skinless
salmon fillets
250g cherry tomatoes
on the vine

1 Preheat the oven to 200°C, fan 180°C, gas mark 6. Line a baking tray with baking paper.

2 Mist a large saucepan over a medium-high heat with cooking spray. Add the onion and garlic and cook, stirring, for 5 minutes or until softened. Add the quinoa and stir, then add 375ml water and bring to the boil. Reduce the heat and simmer, covered, for 10 minutes. Add the asparagus, sugar snaps and peas and cook, covered, for 2-3 minutes, or until the water has evaporated and the vegetables are just tender. Season the pilaf to taste.

3 Meanwhile, put the salmon and tomatoes on the prepared tray. Season to taste. Bake for 10–12 minutes or until the salmon is cooked to your liking and the tomatoes start to collapse. Serve the salmon with the pilaf and tomatoes.

**SmartPoints** values per serving 8
**SmartPoints** values per recipe 32

## 30 MINUTES & UNDER

# Cumin-spiced beef & artichoke kebabs

Serves 4

Prep time
15 minutes

Cook time
15 minutes

Artichokes are an unusual, but delicious, addition to these easy grilled beef kebabs.

## Ingredients

600g sweet potatoes, peeled and chopped
1½ tablespoons garlic-infused olive oil
500g lean sirloin steak, fat trimmed and cut into 3cm pieces
2 teaspoons ground cumin
400g tinned artichoke hearts in water, drained, halved
1 large red onion, cut into 12 pieces
Calorie controlled cooking spray
4 tomatoes, chopped
½ cucumber, chopped
80g reduced-fat feta cheese, crumbled

1 Boil, steam or microwave the sweet potatoes until tender. Drain and mash in a large bowl with 3 teaspoons of the garlic-infused olive oil. Season to taste and cover to keep warm.

2 Meanwhile, preheat your grill to high. Combine the steak, cumin and remaining olive oil in a medium bowl. Thread the pieces of steak, artichokes and onion onto 4 metal or wooden skewers. Mist the kebabs with cooking spray and cook under the grill for 8-10 minutes, turning occasionally, or until the meat is cooked to your liking and the vegetables are tender.

3 Meanwhile, combine the tomatoes and cucumber in a large bowl. Sprinkle with the feta and season to taste. Serve the salad with the skewers and sweet potato mash.

**SmartPoints** values per serving 10
**SmartPoints** values per recipe 38

*Serves 4*

*Prep time*
25 minutes

# Beef pho

A tasty Vietnamese noodle soup with beef steak, bean sprouts, fresh herbs and a spicy chilli kick.

*Ingredients*
200g dried rice noodles
400g beef fillet steak, fat trimmed and very thinly sliced
3 chicken stock cubes (ensure gluten free)
1 tablespoon fish sauce
Juice of 1 lime, plus lime wedges to serve
2 spring onions, thinly sliced
1 small red chilli, deseeded and thinly sliced
150g bean sprouts
Large handful of fresh coriander sprigs

1 Fill and boil the kettle. Put the noodles in a heatproof bowl or large saucepan. Add enough boiling water to cover. Set aside for 10 minutes to soak. Drain and divide among the serving bowls and top with the beef.

2 Put the stock cubes, fish sauce and lime juice in a large heatproof jug or a saucepan. Add 1.5L boiling water and, working quickly, stir to combine and pour over the beef in the bowls. (This piping-hot beef mixture cooks the beef. To make sure it cooks evenly, spread the beef out in the bowls.)

3 Top the pho with the spring onions, chilli, bean sprouts and coriander. Serve with the lime wedges.

**SmartPoints** values per serving 9
**SmartPoints** values per recipe 34

**Try this**

You could serve this with basmati rice on the side – add an extra 3 SmartPoints per 85g serving.

## 30 MINUTES & UNDER

# Fragrant yellow chicken curry

Thai curries are full of flavour and this one is no exception. Use red or green paste, if you like.

**Serves 4**

**Prep time**
13 minutes

**Cook time**
17 minutes

## Ingredients

Calorie controlled cooking spray
1 onion, thinly sliced
600g skinless, boneless chicken thighs, fat trimmed, cut into 2cm pieces
75g yellow curry paste
6 fresh kaffir lime leaves
250ml chicken stock, made with ½ cube (ensure gluten free)
125ml reduced-fat coconut milk
2 carrots, chopped
150g green beans, cut into 3cm lengths
2 teaspoons lime juice
2 teaspoons fish sauce
4 baby pak choi, halved
Small handful of fresh coriander, to garnish

1 Heat a wok over a medium heat. Mist the wok with cooking spray and heat for a further 20 seconds. Add the onion and stir-fry for 5 minutes or until softened. Add the chicken and stir-fry for 2 minutes. Add the curry paste and lime leaves and stir-fry for 1 minute or until fragrant.

2 Add the stock, coconut milk and carrots, and bring to the boil. Reduce the heat and simmer, partially covered, for 5 minutes or until the carrots are almost tender. Add the beans and cook, uncovered, for 3 minutes or until tender. Add the lime juice and fish sauce and stir to combine. Remove and discard the lime leaves.

3 Meanwhile, boil, steam or microwave the pak choi until tender, then drain. Serve the curry garnished with coriander and with the pak choi on the side.

GF

**SmartPoints** values per serving 9
**SmartPoints** values per recipe 37

# Lamb souvlaki

Serves 4

**Prep time**
26 minutes
**Cook time**
4 minutes

Skewers of tender lamb are served with a traditional Greek salad and lightly pickled lettuce.

## Ingredients

400g lean lamb loin fillet,
fat trimmed, cubed
2 teaspoons smoked paprika
1 teaspoon thyme, chopped
2 teaspoons dried oregano
½ iceberg lettuce
1 small red chilli, deseeded
and finely chopped
2 tablespoons white vinegar
1 teaspoon caster sugar
½ teaspoon sea salt flakes
Calorie controlled
cooking spray
200g cherry tomatoes,
1 red pepper, thinly sliced
½ cucumber, thinly sliced
½ red onion, thinly sliced
40g pitted mixed olives
50g reduced-fat feta cheese
4 x 40g wholemeal wraps
60g 0% fat natural
Greek yogurt

1 Combine the lamb, paprika, thyme and half the oregano in a large bowl. Cover and set aside for 15 minutes.

2 Meanwhile, shred the lettuce and combine with the chilli, vinegar, sugar and sea salt in a large bowl. Cover and set aside for 10 minutes, then drain.

3 Mist a griddle pan with cooking spray and preheat over a medium-high heat. Thread the lamb onto 4 metal or wooden skewers. Add the lamb to the pan and cook for 2 minutes each side or until browned and cooked to your liking. Transfer to a plate. Cover the lamb with foil and set aside to rest for 2 minutes.

4 Meanwhile, halve the tomatoes and put in a large bowl with the pepper, cucumber, onion, olives and remaining oregano. Crumble in the feta and mix to combine.

5 Serve the lamb skewers with the wraps, pickled lettuce and Greek salad, with the yogurt on the side.

**SmartPoints** values per serving 15
**SmartPoints** values per recipe 60

# Recipe index

# SmartPoints index